MOTHER NATURE IS TRYING TO KILL ME!

POISONOUS PLANTS

BY JANEY LEVY

Gareth Stevens PUBLISHING

Please visit our website, www.garethstevens.com. For a free color catalog of all our high-quality books, call toll free 1-800-542-2595 or fax 1-877-542-2596.

Library of Congress Cataloging-in-Publication Data

Names: Levy, Janey, author.
Title: Poisonous plants / Janey Levy.
Description: New York : Gareth Stevens Publishing, [2020] | Series: Mother nature is trying to kill me! | Includes bibliographical references and index.
Identifiers: LCCN 2018052203| ISBN 9781538239742 (pbk.) | ISBN 9781538239766 (library bound) | ISBN 9781538239759 (6 pack)
Subjects: LCSH: Poisonous plants–Juvenile literature.
Classification: LCC QK100.A1 L49 2020 | DDC 581.6/59–dc23
LC record available at https://lccn.loc.gov/2018052203

First Edition

Published in 2020 by
Gareth Stevens Publishing
111 East 14th Street, Suite 349
New York, NY 10003

Designer: Sarah Liddell
Editor: Monika Davies

Photo credits: Cover, p. 1 K Steve Cope/Shutterstock.com; background used throughout Zamurovic Photography/Shutterstock.com; p. 4 Stilfehler/Wikimedia Commons; p. 5 Marina Andrejchenko/Shutterstock.com; p. 7 (main) Martin Fowler/Shutterstock.com; p. 7 (inset) dadalia/Shutterstock.com; p. 9 jflin98/Shutterstock.com; p. 11 (main) Svitlana Minazova/Shutterstock.com; p. 11 (inset) Karuna Eberl/Shutterstock.com; p. 13 Greentelect Studio/Shutterstock.com; p. 15 BergelmLicht/Shutterstock.com; p. 17 (main) Schad/Shutterstock.com; p. 17 (inset) vainillaychile/Shutterstock.com; p. 19 Ruud Morijn Photographer/Shutterstock.com; p. 20 L. Braun/Wikimedia Commons; p. 21 (background) egluteskarota/Shutterstock.com; p. 21 (peach pits) Anastasiia Skorobogatova/Shutterstock.com, p. 21 (apple seeds) Roman Samokhin/Shutterstock.com; p. 21 (cherry pits) Valentyn Volkov/Shutterstock.com.

Printed in the United States of America

CPSIA compliance information: Batch #CS19GS: For further information contact Gareth Stevens, New York, New York at 1-800-542-2595.

CONTENTS

Words in the glossary appear in **bold** type the first time they are used in the text.

GRIM GREENERY

Almost everyone likes beautiful flowers. Many people also enjoy gardening and grow flowers, bushes, and trees in their yard. However, did you know some lovely garden plants—and many pretty wild plants—can be deadly?

Some of the plants growing around you produce toxins, or poisons. Some plant toxins cause harm when you touch them. Other plant toxins only hurt you if you eat the poisonous part of the plant. Be careful! Sometimes you can't tell just by looking which plants are poisonous.

PEOPLE SOMETIMES CHOOSE POISONOUS PLANTS FOR THEIR GARDENS BECAUSE OF THEIR BEAUTY. THE HYDRANGEA BUSH IS A BEAUTIFUL PLANT, BUT EATING ANY PART OF IT CAN CAUSE YOU TO **VOMIT** AND HAVE TROUBLE BREATHING.

DEADLY NIGHTSHADE

The name of this plant gives away its killer ability: deadly nightshade. It first grew wild in Europe and Asia. Today, it also grows in gardens in the United States. Every part of the deadly nightshade is toxic, but the sweet berries cause the most poisonings.

THE FORCE OF NATURE

DEADLY NIGHTSHADE IS ALSO KNOWN AS BELLADONNA, WHICH MEANS "BEAUTIFUL LADY" IN ITALIAN. IN THE PAST, WOMEN USED THE PLANT TO MAKE THEIR **PUPILS** LOOK BIGGER, WHICH WAS A POPULAR BEAUTY PRACTICE.

Touching deadly nightshade's leaves can **irritate** your skin. Eating the plant's berries can cause head pain, trouble seeing, problems with thinking, and **convulsions**. In the end, the toxins in the berries might make your heart stop!

EXPERTS SAY EATING AS FEW AS TWO DEADLY NIGHTSHADE BERRIES CAN KILL A CHILD.

WICKED WATER HEMLOCK

Water hemlock is pretty and looks like other plants that are safe to eat. It belongs to the same plant family as carrots and celery. But don't be fooled! This wild greenery is the most toxic plant in North America.

All parts of the plant are toxic, but the roots are the most poisonous. The toxin causes sweating, breathing problems, **seizures**, stomach pain, and vomiting. You might suffer such terrible convulsions that your bones are yanked out of place. Finally, after suffering horribly, you might die.

THE FORCE OF NATURE

THE TOXIN IN WATER HEMLOCK IS VERY STRONG. TAKING A SINGLE BITE OF THE PLANT IS SOMETIMES ENOUGH TO KILL YOU! THE TOXIN CAN CAUSE DEATH WITHIN HOURS.

PEOPLE SAY WATER HEMLOCK'S ROOTS SMELL LIKE CARROTS OR PARSNIPS. THEY SMELL GOOD ENOUGH TO EAT! THAT'S A MEAN TRICK ON THE PART OF THE POISONOUS PLANT.

MENACING MANCHINEEL

The manchineel tree grows from Florida to northern South America, as well as in the Caribbean. This tree has shiny green leaves and fruit that looks like small apples. It's considered Earth's most dangerous tree.

THE FORCE OF NATURE

A SINGLE BITE OF THIS TREE'S FRUIT IS ENOUGH TO PRODUCE SUCH EXTREME PAIN AND SWELLING IN THE THROAT THAT IT'S ALMOST IMPOSSIBLE TO SWALLOW FOOD. THIS CAN HAPPEN WITHIN A COUPLE OF HOURS!

The machineel tree's toxic **sap** runs throughout the tree, including the leaves. Just brushing against the tree can burn your skin! If you set the tree on fire, the smoke may briefly blind you. Eating the fruit can cause such terrible vomiting and **diarrhea** that you die from **dehydration**.

THE FRUIT OF THE MANCHINEEL TREE IS ALSO CALLED THE BEACH APPLE OR THE LITTLE APPLE OF DEATH.

AWFUL OLEANDER

Oleander is a plant with beautiful flowers. It's often grown as a hedge, which is a row of plants that form a border. But don't let this plant's beauty trick you. All parts of the oleander have deadly toxins.

The oleander is so toxic that just touching the plant's leaves or sap can irritate the skin of some people. If you accidentally eat part of the oleander, you may throw up and have diarrhea. Your heart may also be affected. In the end, you might die.

THE FORCE OF NATURE

THE TOXINS IN THE OLEANDER ARE POWERFUL. PEOPLE HAVE GOTTEN SICK EATING HONEY MADE BY BEES THAT ATE THE NECTAR OF OLEANDER FLOWERS!

LUCKILY, THE OLEANDER PLANT TASTES VERY BITTER. ANYONE WHO TRIES TASTING IT ISN'T LIKELY TO EAT VERY MUCH.

MISERABLE MONKSHOOD

Monkshood's pretty blue and purple flowers make it a popular garden plant. But those lovely flowers hide a secret. This is one of the world's deadliest plants!

THE FORCE OF NATURE

YOU MAY START TO SHOW SYMPTOMS, OR SIGNS OF BEING SICK, WITHIN MINUTES OF EATING MONKSHOOD. THERE'S NO **ANTIDOTE** FOR THIS PLANT'S TOXINS. ALL DOCTORS CAN DO IS TREAT YOUR SYMPTOMS.

All parts of monkshood have powerful toxins, some of which can be **absorbed** through your skin. Touching the plant may cause tingling or numbness. If you eat monkshood, you might suffer terrible stomach pain, vomiting, and diarrhea. You may also have trouble breathing and experience changes in your heartbeat. After much pain, some sufferers die.

THE ROOTS OF THE MONKSHOOD CONTAIN THE MOST TOXINS. IF EATEN, THE TOXINS CAN MAKE YOUR HEARTBEAT SLOW DOWN.

KILLER CASTOR BEAN PLANTS

Many gardeners find the castor bean plant quite decorative. It's also a useful plant. The castor bean plant's seeds supply castor oil, which has long been used as a **laxative**. But be careful. After castor oil has been extracted, or removed, from the seeds, the leftover mixture holds one of the world's deadliest toxins: ricin.

The symptoms of ricin poisoning include vomiting, diarrhea, and seizures. These symptoms can last up to a week! Then, after all this terrible suffering, the person often dies.

THE FORCE OF NATURE

IT TAKES VERY LITTLE RICIN TO POISON SOMEONE. IT'S BELIEVED THAT CHEWING OR SWALLOWING JUST A FEW CASTOR BEANS MAY BE ENOUGH TO KILL AN ADULT!

THE CASTOR BEAN PLANT'S DEADLY SEEDS ARE FOUND INSIDE FRUIT. GARDENERS WHO GROW THE PLANT SOMETIMES REMOVE GROWING FRUIT SO NO ONE ACCIDENTALLY EATS THE DEADLY SEEDS.

GHASTLY GIANT HOGWEED

Giant hogweed is a handsome plant that towers over people. It can grow around 13 feet (4 m) tall! This pretty plant has bunches of white flowers that look like umbrellas. But, giant hogweed is a toxic nightmare.

If you touch the sap of giant hogweed, it makes your skin **sensitive** to light. Your skin will then break out in extreme **blisters** if you're out in the sun. And, if you get the plant's sap in your eyes, you're at risk of losing your eyesight!

THE FORCE OF NATURE

IF YOU ACCIDENTALLY TOUCH THE SAP OF GIANT HOGWEED, EXPERTS ADVISE YOU TO QUICKLY WASH THE AREA WITH COLD WATER AND HEAD INSIDE. PUT ON SUNSCREEN IF YOU CAN'T GO INDOORS.

IN THE UNITED STATES, GIANT HOGWEED IS KNOWN AS AN INVASIVE SPECIES, OR A KIND OF LIVING THING LIKELY TO SPREAD AND BE HARMFUL WHEN PLACED IN A NEW AREA.

WHY PLANTS MAKE POISONS

So, why do plants make all these toxins? These deadly plants aren't planning to poison people. They're just trying to stay safe.

Plants can't run from danger. So, plants have had to come up with other ways to protect themselves. They produce toxins to fight off bugs, bacteria, and other living things that would harm them. The toxins also come in handy for protecting plants from animals that might eat them—including people! Like you, plants just want to live!

CYANIDE IS A DEADLY POISON. AND, YOU CAN FIND CYANIDE IN THESE FAMILIAR PLANT SEEDS AND PITS. BUT DON'T WORRY—YOU'D HAVE TO EAT *A LOT* OF EACH SEED OR PIT BEFORE THE POISON HAD ANY EFFECT.

CYANIDE IN SEEDS AND PITS

APPLE SEEDS

GLOSSARY

absorb: to take in
antidote: matter that stops the harmful effects of a poison
blister: a painful swelling on the skin
convulsion: a sudden terrible shaking of the muscles in your body that you can't control or stop
dehydration: the state of having lost too much water
diarrhea: very soft or runny solid waste from a person or animal
irritate: to make part of your body sore or painful
laxative: a medicine or food that makes it easier for solid waste to pass through the body
pupil: the black part in the center of an eye that lets in light
sap: a watery juice inside a plant that carries the plant's food
seizure: a state that's not usual in which you lose awareness of your surroundings and your body moves in an uncontrolled way
sensitive: easily affected by something in a way that is unpleasant or bad
vomit: to have the food or liquid that is in your stomach come out through your mouth because you are sick

FOR MORE INFORMATION

BOOKS

Hicks, Dwayne. *Plants That Poison*. New York, NY: PowerKids Press, 2017.

Lawler, Janet. *Scary Plants!* New York, NY: Penguin Young Readers, 2017.

Schuh, Mari. *Poisonous Plants*. Minneapolis, MN: Pogo, 2019.

WEBSITES

Deadly Nightshade Facts
www.softschools.com/facts/plants/deadly_nightshade_facts/1051/
Learn more facts about the deadly nightshade plant.

Plants
www.dkfindout.com/uk/animals-and-nature/plants
Discover more about how plants grow, the different parts of a plant, and how plants protect themselves.

Poisonous Plants
www.scienceforkidsclub.com/poisonous-plants.html
Read more about poisonous plants on this website.

INDEX